Waterspout

Roisin Flanagan

BookLeaf Publishing

Presentation by *BookLeaf Publishing*

Web: www.bookleafpub.com

E-mail: info@bookleafpub.com

ISBN: 9789357211215

First edition 2022

Presentation by *BookLeaf Publishing*

Web: www.bookleafpub.com

E-mail: info@bookleafpub.com

ISBN: 9789357211215

First edition 2022

For my friends,

whose voices in this matrix were all that mattered.

ACKNOWLEDGEMENT

I would like to thank my father for instilling in me a love of poetry and my mother and sister for believing in my ability to write. I also want to thank all of my English teachers. Your passion was contagious.

PREFACE

Waterspout is a self-validation of overpowering feelings and thoughts. Reading and writing poetry has been a life-preserver for me in the worst times, and I hope it can be for you too.

Heyday

"How are you?"
How am I?
How
Am
I.

I am a cacophony
Of shapes and sounds

Feverish.

There's a gaping wound
In my left side

Septic.

Six million of us
Gone
Forever
Like images reflected off the walls
And furniture
Before the click of the lamp
In the frog hours
Of summer

Like my uncle

Years ago
Improperly
Diagnosed.

They said his cancer was gone
They were wrong.

We're nothing but light
Anyway

I'd like to have thought
The wood was enough
But it doesn't matter
Without air.

I'd like to have thought
My drawings were enough
But when you throw them
In a drawer
They become stuff.

I'd like to have thought
We were enough
But with time
Our souls they'll snuff

Because we're too much.
Because we're too much.

I Have Looked God in the Face

I have looked God in the face
More than once
Deep in my closets
Shoes not worn
In months
And one time in my child
Self
What could I do but
Cough and yelp
And grip the hearts
Of others?

I have looked God in the face
And I see
It is not male
Nor thund'rous
Nor free
It's uneven lines
And it yearns to know me
It is the face
Of my mother.

I have seen God
In Sylvia Plath
Between her bars
Smoke-pits of wrath

Engorged with a burden
Too heavy to bear
She tossed herself off
Tore her life from the snare
And left me here stuck
In the gutters.

Bottom-Feeder

I was swallowed
Last night.
A little death
No one could see
But I.

A death between the breaths
A death between the words
A death between my arm hairs
And the covers.

The problem is
It paralyzes
Prematurely
Embalms
Pin pricks
The crushing
Somnambulism

And it didn't happen
In the dark.
It happened finally at 4 am
With the incandescence
Aware.

I died on everyone's watch.

I died on everyone's watch.

You were there.
You were there.
Yes, you.
How could you?

For it is not loneliness
But rather
It is we
Against
The world.

How we feel too much
How we see too much
How this world is scratch
As it is touch
How it is Dachau
As it is Woodstock
How it is miracle
As it is crock

How we create value
For ourselves

And I
The manta
See in black and white
I have tasted Heaven

Before
And felt my palms brush
Along the floor

Now that I know
What it is to fly
If I stop moving
I will die.

Under God

Americans worship
Things that do not move
A piece of fabric and a copper man
Two lines intersecting
At right angles.
Maybe that's why
A dead Black man
Is more useful to us than
A living one.

The Lakota are more American
Than George Washington's granite head
Looming over a valley
From which he cut his teeth
And when I say valley
I mean slaves

Undocumented immigrants
More American than my uncle
Who felt that their status
Was more important
Than his own soul

Who bows before
Those intersecting lines
As if they could love him

As if they had eaten for him
The mustard that he so viscerally
Detested
When he was seven.

I do not know
What American
Means anymore.

A double negative
A ruination
Of the point

The point being
That we are all here
And we must share each other
And sleep soundly at night.

Fifteen Minutes

When they told me
To wait fifteen minutes
Under observation
I don't think they knew
It was for prayer.

The last time I did it
Was under a bishop's palm
As a 17-year-old
Confirmation attendee.

This time I meant it.

I don't talk to Him anymore.
We were never well acquainted
Never on a first-name-basis
Everything was just so
Formal.

This gym wasn't.
With its uneven lines
And sticky corners
And memories
Of stumbling
And getting up fine.

"You got
The shot"

Four words
Hastily prepared
In block lettering
With shiny stars
Slightly curling
At the edges.

Down to the second
The digits on the far wall
Ticked.

A shudder
Radiated down
From the pin prick.

And I wondered how
They'd spent their last
Fifteen minutes
Which was nothing
Nothing at all
But which was also
A lifetime.

For them
"You lost
The shot"

Would be the banner
Into Paradise.

For them
The shot was much more
Than a single strand
Of RNA

For them
The shot was another day
A full life
A life of joy
A life of pain
And awkwardness and bemusement and
Courage and Love
Which cannot
Possibly
Be summed
In one poem

Now all melted away.

I could only deflate
As I sat on that cold
Metal
Slippery
Sanitized
Chair.
A genuflection

More than I had ever
Made.

The weight
Of all who never
Reached this gym
With its peeling
Stars
And State Champions of '08
Washed over me
And left me unscathed
Save a slight
Right shoulder
Ache.

When my time was done
I held my head up
Threw myself through the doors
And into
The sun.

An Unlikely Pair

We've entered
A state of learned helplessness
Quite the opposite
Of what we've been taught
As Americans
That every input has at least an
Equal output
Which is why some of us struggle
With the unavoidable
The senseless
The apart from
A Greater plan
That we cannot push back against life
When it thrusts itself upon us.
Instead we dare show our faces
And deny
That a single mother
Working three jobs
Below the poverty line
Has suffered
And fought
And loved
And endured.

Caring little for
Each other

Or us
Time and virus
Are locked
In deadly match.

We are propelled
Into the future
Just as violently
As we are pulled
Into a corner.

Time and virus
An unlikely pair
Neither care
Much for how desperately I'd like
An armchair
Or an inviting rock
In the shade.

Unlike me
The sun
Seems to be
A morning person.
It takes everything
To wrench my eyelids open
With each miserable daybreak.

I use to feel the wind
Send tiny kisses

Across my skin
And drink the light
Through my pores
Then conspire
With the violet hue
Of twilight.

Now
I do nothing
So verbose.

I finally admit
I am
Morose.

Life doesn't taste the same
And I don't think
It will ever
Come close.

New York City

A stranger put his arms around me
At Atlantic Avenue Station.
Three feet away
A woman stared
Vacantly forward
Eyes locked on the far wall.

I knew because my eyes were also locked there.

I don't know which came first
The insanity
Or the apathy
The scream
Or the screen
The X-ray vision
Or the tunnel vision

The need to pierce
Or the need to protec

Averages

Remember, men,
Being mean
Is not the mean
Not a reaction
Not a sneeze.
It is a choice
A war to wage
A thrust
Of violence
Onto the world.
The rest know this
Apology
Our peristalsis
And ask each other
To tighten our fists
For even in rage
Our hands
Know only
To hold.

Respect is the mean
Respect is the mean
Respect
Is not
Bold.

To Be Woman

To be woman
Is to be always
Child,
"Don't talk to strangers"
"Don't get in the car"
"Aim for the crotch."

To be woman
Is to fear
Being alone
As if jogging along a dark path
(Hoping for clarity)
Is the same as wandering
A well-lit supermarket
With aisles and aisles
Blurring together
Through tears
And never finding
Mom.

To be woman
Is to fear
The things that go bump
In the night
Believing that
The monsters under the bed

Will disappear
In the morning
When instead
They scramble up the sheets
And lie
Beside you.

To be woman
Is to be
Defined by
Tantrum
When crying is the only way
To cope with
A lack of voice
A guttural sound
Emerging from
The depths
Of history.

We are the lost boys
Who must find
Ourselves

Before it's too late
Dear God
Before it's too late.

Plath

My friend
I have seen your face before
In my mirror
Agate eyes half-empty
Knowing
Knowing

Like Raphael
In the School of Athens.

I have walked with you
Down dimly-lit streets
Lain with you
Cross seldom-tucked sheets
I know
Those shadows
Which seem to twist all around
Till you become
Part of them

Or maybe you always were a shadow
My shadow
A shadow of those before
And after you.

Are you real?
Am I?

All I believe is
I do not believe in anything
But you
Are the voice in my head
And I must say
I am a zealot
And I must pray

For some
Purpose.
I suspect
You have always been here
Watching
Waiting

You see
The world was not
Too much with you
A woman
Who was good at dying

Who was
Better at living
But living is an art
And I am not a painter.

There are two things—
With purpose
And without.

The clock is all
You know
Of time
The thing that
Makes the hours
Ring

A trapped hare
Waits
Or
Ends it all
Before
Its swift
Devouring.

Vaulting Ambition

There is nothing
More dangerous
Than a man
With low self-esteem.

Generation after generation
It is the dissonance
Between that which he is
Encouraged to be
And that which he is.

It is knowing that he is not
And never was
And never will be

Almighty.

It begins at the root
Of the marble curl
And extends past
The radius of the H-bomb.

Indeed, it is old
Yes, even older than Nativity
And it is the greatest lie
Ever told.

Hollowness and Vacancy

I'm not a scrap girl.
I'm the Bitch
Who will walk upright from the table
If not allowed a chair
At the feast.

I'm a tap girl.
Would rather kick than be kicked
Only knows the can-can
And the difference between a foot and a hand
Bends them separately and smiles
For bodies held together by strings
Pinocchios who
Laugh and applaud
With their hands tied.

I was the river and he was the rowboat,
Buoyant
As he dug into me
I bent around him
Curved my lips to comfort him
Not my hips to comfort him
He was on his own course
Tangential to the circle
Of my head
That somehow

Penetrated the folds
Of my brain
But not of my sheets
They've only been wrinkled
By our conversations.

My brows followed suit
In his wake
I lapped
As he rapped
Against my chest
Chipping away at the membranous silences
That filled for him
Through a hole in the hull.

He gently opened
My envelope heart
Tearlessly
Broke into
Without breaking.

This lock-picker
Intimately listened
Coaxed my breast
For each click
Kick, click, kick,
Clicked his teeth
Stroked his beast
And beckoned her to a rib.

Netflix and Chill

You didn't get my favorite movie
And maybe that shouldn't bother me
But
If you have to ask what it meant
That means you didn't feel your heart
Beating out of your chest
A chill send a wave down your arm
Your hairs standing on end
In the light of the TV screen
After which
The only release
Must be to weep.
You decide to prod at the motivations behind the characters
When love was held up naked
For you
It was somehow
Pornographic
And not honest
All you could ask was
"Why did he fuck her?
She is 60 years older than he is"
And what you didn't hear
Was the sound of my heart breaking
Along with Harold's
When she died

When she told him
"Go and love some more"
You chuckled
As if that were some joke
And not truth stripped down
Just having stepped out of the shower
Bearing itself for you
Vulnerable
Patient
Unsubtle
Just as I
Who hated my body
Did for you
Countless times.

If you could accept me,
Why could you not accept her?

Why could you not accept
A woman who knows herself
To be both a splurge
And a necessity?

I wish all women
Knew that we
Are perpetual motion.

Undergrad

We're misunderstood
But we don't misunderstand
We know you've heard
That one before

But when we walk
With arms outstretched
To the parties
We're more than fledglings
More than half-naked
Icaruses
You can see
The stigmata
That mark our worth
If you look under the street lights
Though we try to hide them
Though we try to scrub them off
We have many Xs.

Mine haunt me.
When I see one on campus
I am pierced
In the limbs which he used
Against me
On his body
While I had the obligation to remain

Silent
With the exception of a terse
"It is finished."

These hands
Which I would rather cut off
Than have hold me up
As I slip off a bar

Traitors.

Tell me Caesar was not
Also Brutus.

You think it's a waste
The beers we drink.

You don't know
That they are also chalices of blood
To lubricate
The stones
Bearing down on us
From our fathers.

Why do we forget
That we have all done this?
Killed a part of who we are
To birth our new selves?
Hurled ourselves

Into the air
Before
Cutting ourselves down
And falling back to earth
And our future.

Weed's Dilemma

I will never cry again over someone
Who will never cry about me!

I am perennial!
I’d forgotten
I can make
Essentials
For myself.

I will let no more tears fall
Off my stem
To quench his thirst
Else
He’ll keep drinking up more and more
Of me
Until I’m hollow
Like a bleached limb
Naked
Dry and
Impotent.

No.
The water which passes
Over me
Flows only
Into my own roots.

Like a cactus
I store water
For weeks
And prickle
And bloom
And thrive
In aridness.

More than a poem
I could write books about how
Gentle she is
How miraculous we are
To share
The earth
And our bones
With men.

She made me feel
Like a viper
And a mouse
All at once.

He made me feel
Like his left pinky toenail

He cuts me
And I grow back
To be cut
Again.

Why am I here?

For he is the toenail
Needing me
But forever
Growing
Obsolete.

I am a food chain
Reborn
Of myself.
My roots extend into
My foremothers'
Arms
And history
Is unerasable.

Why am I here?

Why does St. Patrick's Day
Green
Still peek
Between
Dead leaves?

The answer to both questions
Is the same.

The Muse

Once you know what love is
You know what it isn't
Like a horror film
You can't unsee
Frankenstein's monster
Etherized upon a table.

I was what you might call
A critic.

I knew how someone should be loved
I knew how someone could be loved
But
That's drifting through a gallery
Instead of painting.

I could see his arms
In the dim kitchen light
At 1:16
He put his keyboard
On the table.

His fingers arched
Toward god
Or knowledge
But not toward me

Even though he was standing
In the middle of my house

And I understood—
Art is greater than
Other people.

What I understand now
Is that art is other people
And no one
Wants to die alone
Clutching a
Hunk of metal
And wiring.

I water-colored a lily
At thirteen
And was almost convinced I was Monet
He never watered his lilies either.

I sketched my grandmother
Without looking into her eyes.

Unlike the man standing
In the middle of my house
She understood that

Shadows are blue
Not black

That's why a baby cries

Before adaptation
Dulls the senses
And art becomes
Everything
And the muse
Becomes
Nothing.

Grammy,
Monet,
And I
Our bones collapsing into the earth
Instead of hanging in a foyer
We bellow under the hands
Of time.

Ode to Lear

In shadow I stride
I'm petrified
As the wood
In which I reside
Rings and wrinkles
Adorn me
As I reach the sky
Plants arch around my head
And into my brain
Doubts
Debts
Daughters

Stock-holders
Pinching around my neck
For comfort

The wolf's tooth
Breaks into a crown
Cuckoos frown
Fledglings
Darkling
By the moon
Begotten of me
Yet not of me

Mothers
Murderers
Mirrors
As I reflect
Mist and rain drown me
In a warm embrace
Wind blows kisses across
My white crest
Mother Nature is fair
She wrenches not
But bequeaths
To all
A love
Unconditional

"I am the king himself"
Yet not of himself
"They told me I was everything" but
I am a king "of nothing."

"Nothing can come of nothing"

Yet something
Alights in darkness
A butterfly
Migrates south
From nothing
Opens the cage
Of nothing

Deforms the bars
Around nothing
Shatters Nothing's
Egg
And germinates tearfully
Into the storm
Filling the cracks
And crow's feet
With nothing

"No cause, no cause," says she.

Cause wants effect
Entitlement
Title
Given or inborn?
Taken or earned?
I learned
Too late
I was the Fool.

"Old fools are babes again"!
And babes are fools
"My poor fool is hang'd!"
"Pinned and wriggling on the wall"
Confined to a crib
Gilded and swaddled
In nothing

My eyes
Pared on both sides
Cannot spy
But by Fortune,
“God’s spies”
Need none.

Erosion

Upon the beach
Of Lake Ontario
Flecks of color are scattered intermittently
Among the rock
Which has been churning
Over millions of years

The beach glass
More or less
Twenty.

It is a combination of
Industry
And nature
Forged not out of
Bubbling and scraping
From the dark and mystifying center
Of the earth
(Which somehow contains light
In our dreams)
But of the loving stroke
Of water
And factory workers

And it doesn't hurt your feet.

We've been here
One minute to midnight.

Like beach glass
We are synthetic
And natural-born swimmers
And when you distill us down
Over time
You get something
Quite different
Than the manufacturer intended

But you and I will become soft
And shriveled
Not dull.
We rust.

Beauty
For us
Is not smooth
It never was.

And Explosion

My father almost drowned
In a riptide
Before I was born.
His savior
Was a skittish yet plucky teenager
With a plastic surf board.

He had trodden water
For hours
Reminding himself
To just stay afloat
"That's all you have to do
Stay afloat
Potential energy is survival."

Sink
Your head
Below the surface
Of a yellow-bottomed
Lake in summer
At dusk
When the dragonflies
Alight on everything
That is still

Remember when water

Was your friend.

Somehow
Soon
We burst forth
We always do

I suspect
Even at the end.

Waterspout

I watched a spider dance
On the ceiling of our tent
While lightning struck all around us
And suddenly I realized
I had more in common
With her
Her spindly legs scrambling
Across the nylon
I caught my breath
And imagined our hairs standing on end
Before
Dying
He, she, and I
At least it would be quick

But then I remembered my father
Forty years before
In the same blanket
We wore now
Keeping alive
In the mud
And cold
And oblivion
Of the Army
I remembered my hippie mother
Who had made airplane turbulence

Into a roller coaster
A dark crevice
Into a hidey-hole

Then I remembered
How unlikely lightning strike is
I remembered dozens of children
Yards away
At their own sites
Were more scared
Than I
I imagined my someday daughter
Afraid of the same lightning
And I held that little girl tight

"Isn't this fun?"
And she smiled
And I smiled
And he leaned into me
And the spider was still.

Epiphany

The first time
I thought I was dying
Was when our canoe
Tipped over
At age five.

You can imagine
The way my plum-sized heart
Almost exploded
Watching my
Peanut-butter
And jelly
Drifting
Resolutely
To the bottom
Before vanishing
Into the dark.

My father was nowhere.
For a split-second
It was only I
Who for the first time
In my disposable camera life
Understood what alone meant.

Until then
I moved my arm
And it obeyed
Or I asked my mother to move hers
And she obeyed.

But the wind that day
Would move its arm
Of its own volition
With a violence
I did not know
A hand could wield.

The water meanwhile
Could only yield
It seemed to struggle
With my weight.
Were it not for my life-jacket
I would have found myself
Gasping
Being let down
Without asking.

A rock jutting
Out of the water
Unexpectedly
Scratched me
As not even a sister could
In wrestling.

My father was
Of course
A few yards away
Bobbing up and down
Like a buoy
A lighthouse
A talisman.

The elements had been much kinder
To him.

Keeping himself afloat
With nothing
He reached out a limb.

And I learned loneliness
Evolves.
First, it is treading water
Then, it is standing
In a crowded room.

And I learned pain
Evolves.
First, it is external
Then, it is a deep
Soul-wound.

And I learned fear
Evolves
First, it is for oneself
Then, it is for one's crew.

And I learned love
Evolves.
First, it is the air we breathe
Then, it is a pearl
We dive for.

One we would die for.

www.ingramcontent.com/pod-product-compliance
Lightning Source LLC
Chambersburg PA
CBHW051737130826
49812CB00033B/894
* 9 7 8 9 3 5 7 2 1 1 2 1 5 *